THL
ABOUT THE
DA VINCI CODE
ANSWERS FOR CATHOLICS

The seats in the courthouse were uncomfortable, and the movie they showed us was terrible. The basic plot: A husband had been called for jury duty and was trying to weasel out of it. "John," his wife scolded, "participating in jury duty is a great civic responsibility." I looked around the room at my fellow citizens, who, with me, had been called to duty that

The Truth About The Da Vinci Code: Answers for Catholics
was written by editor-in-chief Daniel Connors with the editorial staff of *Catholic Digest*. ©2006 *Catholic Digest*. All rights reserved. Printed in U.S.A.

1

day. Few were even watching the film.

Then the movie switched to the chief justice of my state, who gave us a quick history of the jury system, including the Magna Carta, that foundation of English liberty that the "people made King John sign while he was filling in for good King Richard, who was away on the Crusades." I winced. Richard had been dead for 16 years when the Magna Carta was signed. Evidently the chief justice of my state gets his history from Robin Hood movies. As do most of us.

With a few notable exceptions, serious historians just don't write best sellers like they used to. Today most of us get our history from novelists and from Hollywood — where, unlike the jury system of my state, they know how to tell exciting, convincing stories.

Books and movies: good and bad
This isn't all bad, by any means. You can learn a lot about ancient Rome from the novels and film adaptations of Robert Graves (*I Claudius*), medieval England from the Brother Cadfael mysteries of Ellis Peters, and the Civil War from the novels of Shelby Foote. And the same with movies. *Shakespeare in Love* can give us helpful images of life in London in the early 1600s. Franco Zeffirelli's *Romeo and Juliet* gives us a view of life in Renaissance Italy, Mel Gibson's *Braveheart* gives us an indelible picture of the Scottish highlands in the late 14th century, and *Midway* strives to give us an accurate image of Americans and Japanese at war in the Pacific.

But books and movies also can plant less helpful images in our minds that are hard to shake and that can do harm to the historical record or to our view of other people. Native Americans are justly irritated by their portrayal in many early Hollywood westerns. African-Americans see Prissy, the African–American maid in *Gone With the Wind*, or the number of Hollywood movies and TV shows in which they play only drug dealers and pimps; they hardly are consoled by the thought that it's only a movie.

Images and ideas that come to us through powerful storytelling tend to stay with us and help us define ourselves, others, and our world. Even Robert Langdon, Dan Brown's hero in *The Da Vinci Code*, recognizes the power of movie images. Early in the book, when he tries to convince a French detective that the pentacle is not a demonic  symbol, the detective counters that it must be, since it shows up as one in so many American horror movies — leaving Langdon to mutter to himself, with evident sarcastic irritation, "Thank you, Hollywood."

Thanks a lot, *Da Vinci Code*!

Today, a lot of Christians find themselves expressing the same sarcastic irritation as the fictional Robert Langdon. "Thank you, Dan Brown; thank you, Hollywood." *The Da Vinci Code* sat atop *The New York*

Times bestseller list for months. Some 43 million hard-cover copies have been sold. And with its plot premise that Mary Magdalene was pregnant with Jesus' child at the time of the Crucifixion and moved to France, where their daughter gave birth to a line of French royalty, and that the Church covered it all up, the book has come under serious fire from Christians of every stripe, who, in a counter-avalanche of books, magazine articles, and Web sites, have attacked it for being everything from blasphemous and a sin to read to just plain silly. And now, the movie.

So, what should we do?
How should Catholics deal with this huge phenomenon? How should we talk about it with our children, non-Catholics, non-believers? What should we make of it, especially with the movie being seen now by millions? Should we imitate the crowds on Good Friday in Mel Gibson's *Passion* shouting "crucify," only this time referring not to Christ but to Brown and Hollywood? Or should we be like King Arthur in *Monty Python and the Holy Grail* (incidentally, *my* favorite Grail film) and shout "Run away, run away!"?

No, we at *Catholic Digest* think a healthy Catholic response lies somewhere else: in knowledge, in understanding, and in getting in touch with our own faith. So let's begin with some premises that are worth exploring, move on to some samples of just how reliable or unreliable Brown's premises are, suggest two topics that need to be part of any discussion of the story, and then recommend some resources that can help.

10 KEY POINTS
for putting *The Da Vinci Code* in context

As we read, watch, or hear about *The Da Vinci Code*, how should Catholics understand and react? Here are ten key points that can help us all deal with the story and grow in our faith.

1 It's here and it does present a challenge.

For many readers the book is an exciting page-turner. It's a mystery, and people love mysteries. It's full of puzzles, and people love to solve puzzles. It's got heroes and villains, and for a long while we're not sure which is which. It feeds into our cultural assumption that institutions are not to be trusted, an assumption recently fed, among Catholics and non-Catholics alike, by some Church leaders trying to cover up incidents of clergy sex abuse. As characters in the book say at least twice, everybody loves to uncover a conspiracy.

Even more, *The Da Vinci Code* relies on our basic cultural ignorance of our own Christian story. And while its historical analysis is as fictional as the characters (see page 16), its premise of a male-dominated Church suppressing the "sacred feminine" plays well in a culture that often sees the Church as not really treating women as equals.

Other novels and pseudo-histories have explored these topics before, but Brown's page-turner hit at the right time. Word-of-mouth reports spread sales — and the furor raised by Christians surely didn't hurt the well-tuned publicity machine either. Lots of people we know may be affected by it, especially if they are feeling alienated from, or angry with, the Church.

2 Since the Resurrection, Christians themselves (not to mention their non-Christian opponents) have differed in how they understood Jesus and his mission and message.

The Da Vinci Code uses some of these differences as an important piece of its entire plot. Some of the disputes in the early Church make today's squabbles look very tame in comparison. For example:

- **Divisions in the New Testament.** Right in the New Testament we see Christians who felt gentiles had to become Jews before they could be Christians. And we have St. Paul arguing much the opposite.
- **Divisions in the early Church.** In the first few centuries we have Ebionites: Jewish vegetarian Christians who accepted only the Gospel of Matthew because it was the most Jewish of the Gospels (and by changing one letter in the word

for *locusts* they changed John the Baptist's menu to pancakes and wild honey, in keeping with their vegetarian ideals).

- **Weighing old against new.** Before the year 200 we have Marcion, who felt the God of the Old Testament was so different from the God of Jesus that the two were not the same God. He threw out the Old Testament and kept only an edited version of Luke and some of Paul's letters.

- **Was Jesus adopted?** We have adoptionist Christians, who felt Jesus was born human and was infused with divine power only at his Baptism, when the Holy Spirit descended ("This is my beloved Son," the voice from heaven says. "Today I have begotten You.") Jesus was, in other words, adopted by God the Father.

- **Can God suffer?** We had Christians who came to be called Docetists (from the Greek word for *appear*), who believed Jesus was fully God and only appeared to be human and only appeared to die on the Cross — because, they argued, God could not suffer.

3 **Of all these groups of early Christians, none are more important for Dan Brown's novel than the groups known as Gnostics.** Gnosticism is an umbrella term for a huge and extremely complex movement in Greco-Roman culture that affected a lot of people in the early centuries after Jesus. Many early Christians were

affected by Gnostic thinking.

Gnosticism is very hard to explain adequately in a short space, and individual groups of Gnostics didn't always agree on what it meant. In general, Gnostics believed in a number of divinities called *aeons*, living in a heavenly realm called the *Pleroma*. There was trouble in heaven, as there often is in mythology, and a bad aeon managed to break up the female aeon Sophia and scatter her over a newly created earth. These divine sparks came to rest in individuals, who needed to access secret wisdom and knowledge (*gnosis* is the Greek word for knowledge) in order to free the divine spark in them, so it could ascend to the Pleroma, its true home. This secret, esoteric knowledge was the source of salvation.

Some Gnostic groups seem to have given women a more equal role with men than orthodox Christians did; other Gnostics, however, saw women as the root of all evil (especially in regard to sexual temptation).

This secret knowledge would be disclosed by a revealer who would descend from the Pleroma's (heaven's) realm of light. He would help those who had the divine spark within them understand that their true home is not in this evil world but in the light, a place to which he would return. For Gnostic Christians, Christ was the revealer, the aeon sent to impart this secret knowledge of salvation. Gnosticism was also, in a sense, an elitist religious philosophy — not everybody had this divine spark.

We know from the Gnostics' own writings that because the most important thing was to free the divine spark from the body, they tended to be very anti-materialist. The body was not something to be fed and pleasured, but something to be punished and got free from. (This is an important point for readers of *The Da Vinci Code*, which seems to want to imply just the opposite.)

4 Points 2 and 3 lead us to realize that the history of the Church is far more complex, and actually far more interesting, than the conspiracy theory Brown's characters propose.

Among the Gnostics, Docetists, Ebionites, Marcionites, and many other expressions and understandings of Jesus, his message, and the Church, there were, of course, those Christians who eventually would come to be seen as the orthodox — the "right thinkers." But imagine their challenge: The apostolic generation was gone, there was no Magisterium as we think of it today, no *Catechism of the Catholic Church* to guide them. There wasn't even a collection of apostolic writings (what became the New Testament) that everybody agreed upon until some four hundred years after Jesus (for more on this see point 5, below).

Imagine yourself in their position: How do you

stay on the right track? What interpretations of Jesus are outside the boundaries, and where are the boundaries to begin with? After two thousand years of doctrinal development we forget that they didn't know the answers. They didn't know how their story would come out. The Church, believing it ultimately was being led by the Spirit, worked out basic understandings through discussion, debate, conflict (sometimes bitter and violent), and yes, votes. (Vatican II had votes, Vatican I had votes, the Council of Trent had votes, earlier councils all had votes. Sophie Neveau in *The Da Vinci Code* expresses shock at the idea of a vote, but there should be nothing shocking or surprising about it.)

5 In the novel, Sophie Neveau is shocked to hear that the Church created the New Testament. This is true: The New Testament we know today was not developed as a unit, and it didn't develop quickly.

This point was made over and over in past times by Catholics defending the Church against the Protestant notion that Scripture is the only guide. The Church, these old defenders responded, came first. The Church wrote the Scripture. The Church decided what books would be included in the New Testament.

At first, there was no Christian Scripture at all. There was the Old Testament. The Church's biblical scholars believe that the Gospels of Matthew, Mark, Luke, and John were written in different places at different times, sometime between 30 and 60 years after the Resurrection. In the early days it is very possible that a particular Christian community had nothing but oral stories of Jesus or the Apostles, or a letter or two from Paul, or maybe just Luke's Gospel or John's or Matthew's or Mark's.

Fairly quickly, however, we find early Christians quoting these four Gospels or one of Paul's letters in a way that tells us they were seeing them as Scripture — sacred, inspired by God, normative, on a par with the Old Testament. Certainly by the year 200 A.D. Matthew, Mark, Luke, and John had acquired prominence in most Catholic communities. But debates would go on for another 200 years about what other writings should

Athanasius, bishop of Alexandria, was the first to propose exactly the list of 27 books we have in the New Testament. Writing to his parishes in 367 A.D., he said, "In these alone the teaching of godliness is proclaimed. Let no one add to these; let nothing be taken away."

be considered Scripture. How about the document known as Paul's *Letter to the Laodiceans*, or the Book of Revelation? Some wanted to include the Wisdom of Solomon, which is now part of the Catholic *Old* Testament.

There were some books that were given scriptural

status in some parts of the Church but not in others. One of the oldest bound copies of the New Testament we have, from the fourth century, contains all 27 books that we know as the New Testament, but it also contains the *Shepherd of Hermas* and the *Letter of Barnabas* — fascinating books that eventually didn't make the final cut.

Eventually the Christian community — that part that would later be known as the orthodox — developed criteria for judging whether a book should be included as Scripture, or revered as non-scriptural Christian writing (for example, the *Shepherd of Hermas* and the letters of Clement), or excluded entirely. Athanasius of Alexandria, late in the fourth century, is the first person we know of to propose the list containing all 27 books we know as the New Testament, and nothing but those 27 books. (And it's interesting to note, *Da Vinci Code* fans, that Athanasius proposed his list some 30 years after the novel says Constantine made the choices, and many years after Constantine's own death).

6 A good storyteller asks us to suspend our disbelief and enter into the story he or she tells. But... (continued in no. 7)

There is nothing wrong with suspending our disbelief

to enter into a story. We need to believe, at least as long as the story lasts, that lions can talk, dragons breathe fire, warriors fly through the sky in spacecraft, toy spacemen can cry "To infinity and beyond!," or, as in another recent movie, *National Treasure*, there's a coded map on the back of the Declaration of Independence that tells the location of the treasure of the Knights Templar.

Suspending our skeptical faculties is all part of the fun.

7 But... if a storyteller wants us to believe that his or her story is not fiction, but true, he or she needs to provide evidence.

Please note well: *An opinion is not evidence.* A storyteller can tell us Mary and Jesus were married and opened a crepe shop on the French Riviera where they entertained space aliens and sent their daughter to the Sorbonne, but if the storyteller wants us to believe this is *true*, he or she needs to give us evidence. And saying the Church doesn't want you to know something is not evidence that somebody's theory is true — even if he gives you evidence that the Church truly doesn't want you to be affected by the theory.

8 The story of our faith is worth exploring, and questioning is a necessary part of growing in faith.

We should never be afraid of questions. They can

lead us to deeper answers, deeper involvements in Christian living, and deeper connections to the Church. Asking questions can be scary. We don't always know where the answers will take us. But we trust in Christ — that is what faith is all about — that our spiritual quest that begins in Him, will end in Him. And don't forget that the Church says that faith and reason go hand in hand. Since God is the author of all truth, whether revealed or reasoned, there can be no ultimate conflict.

The Da Vinci Code shows us fictional people on a fictional quest for truth. Our quest is real, and in the long run can be more challenging and exciting than anything Robert and Sophie experience in the book or movie.

9 *The Da Vinci Code*, for all its faults, can inspire Catholics to ask good questions about their faith — though the answers clearly will have to be found elsewhere.

Some of the best questions that *The Da Vinci Code* can inspire us to ask ourselves are: *Who really is Jesus? What place does He have in my life? If I really believe in Him, what does that mean for how I live my life, or for my involvement with the Church?*

All these questions stem from a crucial question that Jesus Himself asked the disciples, and us by extension: "And you: Who do you say that I am?"

In some ways, who we are as the Church, as a parish, as individual believers, all the doctrine we've ever developed, come back to Jesus' central question: "Who do you say that I am?"

10 There are answers!

Christians again and again have found that there are no better, more reliable, more fully rounded sources of answers to our questions about Jesus than the four Gospels known as Matthew, Mark, Luke, and John. And the Catholic Church has had two thousand years of experience exploring the boundaries of biblical interpretation. This doesn't mean the Church can't come to new insights about Jesus and his message and mission, but it does mean that the Church is the best guide we have for making sure our own interpretations don't go beyond boundaries that were worked out with such effort over so many centuries.

These ten key points strike us as critically important for Catholics who want to put *The Da Vinci Code* into context. If Dan Brown has piqued your interest, that's great! But even if your adventure starts with him, there are important reasons not to let your journey end with him, as the next section shows.

FACT OR FICTION?
A quick summary

FACT: *The Da Vinci Code* is full of historical error.

What is Dan Brown really up to? He starts off with a "fact" page, which clearly gives the impression that the history he's going to give and the documents he's going to cite are all real and factually accurate. Then, throughout the book he weaves a history that a high school student could tear to pieces in just a half hour on the Internet. If he is trying to really convince us of his Grail theory, why would he build it on such shoddy evidence? Why wouldn't he take the short amount of time it would have taken just to fix the worst of the amateurish blunders? Did he intend his history to be as fictional as his characters? Did he do such a bad job deliberately so that Christian critics would hammer him gleefully and thus generate even more publicity and sales? I don't know. Maybe he was just out to tell a good story and made up the details, the way a *Star Trek* episode needs a certain amount of nonsensical-but-right-sounding techno-babble.

In any case, babble is generally what Brown has given us. And we need to be able to say that without sounding defensive.

Examples? Entire books have been written correcting the sloppy errors in *The Da Vinci Code*. There are so many errors of fact that a debunker can quickly start sounding mean-spirited, but we do need to give at least a taste of Brown's factual errors if we're going to place his novel into a proper context. So, for example...

1. Constantine. Virtually everything Brown says about Constantine and his era in this novel is either completely wrong or seriously flawed. For example, Brown's character Sir Leigh Teabing says that Constantine "was a lifelong pagan." The historical record, however, tells us that Constantine's conversion to Christianity was most probably genuine. He *was* baptized on his deathbed, as Teabing says, but so were many Christians of that time. Being baptized on one's deathbed was not uncommon in an age when the frequent Sacrament of Penance was unknown. To sin after Baptism was dangerous: At most you might have one more chance at being forgiven. An emperor, whose job was not exactly holy, wouldn't want to have his sins forgiven too early. The Church didn't like this practice, but it happened.

Teabing tells us that Christians were multiplying exponentially at the time of Constantine, and wars between pagans and Christians had grown to such proportions that it "threatened to rend Rome in two." Historians, however, scratch their heads at this. When Constantine converted, Christians numbered about 8 percent of the total empire, and the "war" was all one way: For the 250 years before Constantine, the tiny minority of Christians had been sporadically persecuted, hunted down, arrested, tortured, and put to death. The worst period of persecution was probably most of the ten years before Constantine's conversion.

Constantine never unified Rome under the single religion of Christianity, as Teabing asserts. Constantine did make Christianity legal in 313 A.D., but it didn't become the official religion of the empire until some 50 years after his death.

2. The Council of Nicea.

Constantine died a long time ago. Who cares? But the stakes go up as Brown looks at the Church Council of Nicea, which Constantine convened in 325 A.D.

Brown's character Leigh Teabing says that, until the Council of Nicea, "Jesus was viewed by his followers as a mortal prophet, a great and powerful man, but a man nonetheless... Jesus' establishment as the 'son of God' was officially proposed and voted on by the council of Nicaea."

Whether you care about Constantine or not, it's crucially important for Catholics to know that what Brown has Teabing saying here is pure baloney. Teabing's assertion that Jesus was seen as a mere man until the Council of Nicaea in the year 325 A.D. would have come as a surprise to St. Paul, who, 20 years after the Crucifixion, was already using the word "God" to describe Jesus. It would come as a surprise to the writers of the Gospels and early Christian writings outside of the New

Testament, who speak of Jesus as God.

There were, however, very powerful and sometimes violent struggles in the early Church about how to understand Jesus as God. Was Jesus exactly the same as God the Father? Did God the Father die on the Cross? Was Jesus praying to Himself when He said "Our Father..."? Was Jesus born human and then infused with divinity when the Holy Spirit came down at his Baptism? Was He fully God but only appeared to be human? And how can there be only one God if Jesus and the Father were both God, and how does the Holy Spirit fit into this?

Thomas answered Jesus and said, "My Lord and my God." (John 20:28)

Remember: We have the benefit of the *Catechism of the Catholic Church* today only because these early Christians did the very hard work of thinking these questions through. Many held differing ideas that had to be resolved. But the idea that Christians before Nicea understood Jesus as just a man, or that "Constantine turned Jesus into a divinity," as Teabing adds, are just plain wrong.

3. The Gnostic texts. In the novel Leigh Teabing backs up his claims about the Church making Jesus divine by speaking of documents uncovered in 1945 in Nag Hammadi, Egypt. "In addition to telling the true Grail story," Teabing says, "these documents speak of Christ's ministry in very human terms."

The discovery of the Nag Hammadi manuscripts is, indeed, very important for understanding early Christianity. The cache included 46 different books, most of which had never been seen or were known only because they were quoted by early Church Fathers who were attacking their ideas. Most are clearly works of various Gnostic Christian groups who were considered heretical by what became orthodox Christianity. They include books that call themselves gospels, such as the *Gospel of Philip*, along with treatises and mythological works that on the whole were written long after the four Gospels we have in our New Testament.

The problem for Teabing and Brown is that, if anything, Jesus appears far more supernatural in these texts than He does in any of our four Gospels (in which He grows weary, hungry, thirsty, bleeds, and dies). There is truly very little, if anything, in the Nag Hammadi books to back up an idea that the Church suppressed evidence of Jesus' humanity. If anything, it shows that the orthodox Church fought hard to hold on to Jesus' humanity. Don't take our word for it. These Nag Hammadi documents have been translated into English and are readily available (see "Seeking the Truth," page 28).

Teabing says Jesus' "life was recorded by thousands of followers across the land.... More than 80 gospels were considered for the New Testament."

Actually, there is no evidence anywhere that Jesus even had thousands of followers in his lifetime. And careful scholarship points out that, in the most literate of places in the empire at that time, no more than 15 percent of the people could read at all or sign their names, never mind write fluently.

We are aware of other books calling themselves gospels, but a dozen or so, surely not 80. There are fanciful stories of Jesus' childhood where He makes live birds out of clay and lengthens a board that Joseph had cut short so that his stepfather wouldn't lose a contract.

There are gospels full of Jesus' "secret sayings" (a basic tenet of Gnosticism was that there is secret knowledge that leads to salvation). Although a few of these gospels may contain elements that come from very early Christian times, they have been put into such a very strong Gnostic context (which really didn't start to infiltrate Christian communities until well after Christ's death and Resurrection) that it's impossible to know what is early and what isn't — making these gospels much farther removed from Jesus' time than anyone suggests for Matthew, Mark, Luke, and John.

4. Were Jesus and Mary married? The whole plot of *The Da Vinci Code* revolves around the notion that Jesus and Mary Magdalene were married and that Mary was pregnant with their child at the time of the Crucifixion. Mary, Leigh Teabing argues, is the real Holy Grail. This is

proven, he says, especially by the Gnostic books called the *Gospel of Philip* and the *Gospel of Mary*. Teabing goes on to say: "Jesus entrusted his mission to Mary Magdalene rather than to Peter ... The church, to defend itself against the Magdalene's power" smeared her reputation and "perpetuated her image as a whore ..."

Is there any truth in any this? Scholars clearly say no — on all counts.

It is true that Mary Magdalene often has been characterized as a former prostitute in pious writings and sermons over the centuries, but a careful reading of the New Testament shows that Matthew, Mark, Luke, and John *never* say that. In fact, all four of our Gospels give Mary an exalted position as the apostle to the Apostles, the first witness to the Resurrection, and the one who brought the good news to the male disciples. Why would the Church have kept such passages in the New Testament if it was trying to smear her or "defend itself against her power"?

To be fair to Brown and his fictional historian, the fragmentary *Gospel of Mary* and the *Gospel of Philip* do give Mary Magdalene a prominence among the disciples that she doesn't have in the New Testament. In the third-century *Gospel of Mary*, the male disciples express some jealousy that Jesus seems to be favoring her with special teaching. But this is still a long way from claiming Mary and Jesus were married and had a child. And nowhere, in any document discovered anywhere, is there even a hint that Jesus entrusted his mission to Mary instead of to Peter.

The *Gospel of Philip* is a strange book of Gnostic

teaching and very difficult for even scholars to make sense of. It does speak of the Magdalene as the one "whom they call [the Lord's] lover." But three paragraphs later it says "God is a man eater. On account of this the Man was killed for him. Before they killed the Man they killed animals, for those were not Gods for whom they killed." One needs to be be very careful drawing conclusions about what any passage in *Philip* might mean.

The New Testament indicates that at least some of the disciples, including Peter, were married. If Jesus had been married, what would be the point of hiding it? Brown is wrong when he argues that an unmarried Jewish man would have been unthinkable — we know some Jews chose celibacy for religious reasons.

Brown is not the first writer to imagine a relationship between Jesus and Mary Magdalene, and doubtless he won't be the last. But, based on anything that has ever been discovered, there isn't one shred of evidence anywhere that they were married, despite what Brown's characters assert.

5. The fact page. As we said before, there are many excellent books detailing Brown's factual errors and baseless assertions. And nobody would probably care if Brown hadn't stated on a "fact" page that all documents, etc., mentioned in the book are factual.

The "fact" page also talks about a medieval society known as the Priory of Sion. French reporters have pointed out that the Priory of Sion was founded in 1956 by André Bonhomme, Pierre Plantard, and two of their

23

friends, who still constitute the total membership.

Dan Brown's fact page is fiction. That's not our *opinion* — it's a fact.

6. Leonardo's painting. So after all this, what about the story of Leonardo's painting of the Last Supper? Is the red-haired figure Mary Magdalene? Leonardo didn't paint name tags on the figures in his painting, so isn't Brown as entitled to his opinion as anybody else?

In a sense, sure. Leonardo isn't here to testify so we can't *prove* that it isn't Mary. But since Brown's entire case leading up to the painting is so fatally — not to mention sloppily — flawed, why give his argument more credence than centuries worth of careful art historians and interpreters who almost universally argue that the figure is John? In the context of other Leonardo drawings of young men, it is not surprising that John, thought to be the youngest of the disciples, would have a feminine appearance. John also often was depicted as clean-shaven.

Brown may be entitled to his opinion on this, but, as we said, opinion is not evidence. So why should we be swayed by an opinion based on no credible evidence at all? We don't believe every diet claim we read. We don't give our money to every overseas attorney who contacts us by e-mail promising to reward us handsomely for our help in transferring his client's zillion dollars to a U.S. bank. In much the same way, Brown gives us no credible reason, anywhere, to see his book as anything but fiction.

DISCUSSING THE DA VINCI CODE
Two critical points

Some opinions are more worthy of belief than others.

A friend of mine teaches theology at a Catholic college in New York State. A couple of years ago he lamented to me that his students didn't trust anything the Church said, but they believed that everything they saw on *The X-Files* was true. Such an attitude can make discussions of *The Da Vinci Code* very difficult.

Whom do we trust?

Since the 1960s and '70s, distrust of institutions and authority has become a common and almost unconsciously accepted part of our culture. The bigger the institution, the more some of us instinctively distrust it. And, yes, sometimes big institutions (just like little institutions and individuals) do try, often ineptly, to hide some truths.

This is an important topic for any families, friends, co-workers, or groups that find themselves discussing *The Da Vinci Code* novel or movie. There is something inside many of us that wants to believe we've been lied to: that the moon landings were faked or that our government is really in touch with aliens. Someone proposes a conspiracy theory and, no matter how kooky, some of us will go "Hmm ... of course!"

We all have a right, and a need, to be skeptical. Every day we're bombarded with huge amounts of information and advertising, all trying to convince us what to believe and what to buy. Spin is in, but so are well-meaning people who believe that what they are saying, retelling, or forwarding is true. Spending even a little time browsing on the urban legends Web site snopes.com can be a real eye-opener. The problem, as the old saying goes, isn't with what we don't know. It's with what we think we know that just isn't so.

Brown's writing is more lively than that of most professional historians, but "lively" isn't the same as "credible."

Any discussion of *The Da Vinci Code* that goes beyond its entertainment value needs to touch upon this issue of trust and distrust. Should we automatically assume that the Church has successfully hidden truths for 2,000 years, until Dan Brown revealed the secrets? Why is is so difficult for some to give the Church the benefit of the doubt, and so easy to believe a novelist who tells us a whopper like "Constantine chose what gospels would be in the New Testament ... among them Matthew, Mark, Luke, and John"? Not only did Constantine have nothing to do with choosing the books of the New Testament, but what is this *"among them"*? There aren't any other gospels in the New Testament. So what makes Brown more credible for some people than all the honest and careful biblical scholarship of the Church?

My opinion, your opinion

A second topic that would make for great family discussion is the cultural notion that everyone is entitled to his or her opinion. This, of course, is true: This is a democracy, and we at *Catholic Digest* are grateful to live in a country where no one can tell us what we must think or believe or say. The problem isn't with this notion but with one that often rides on its coat tails: Because everyone is entitled to his or her opinion, every opinion must be equally valid and valuable.

Really? First of all, it's hard to see how facts may be open to legitimate differences of opinion. If they were, they wouldn't be facts. When Brown says the Dead Sea Scrolls were discovered in the 1950s, he's not stating a legitimate opinion. He's just plain wrong. When he says the Priory of Sion is a secret medieval society, he is not stating a legitimate opinion, because it clearly isn't true. In the same way, should we give any credence to a person who opines that Christopher Columbus sailed the ocean blue in 1962? We hope not.

So, when an opinion is supposedly based on facts, but clearly isn't, what makes that opinion so attractive to so many people? Why not explore that question with your parents, children, spouse, friends, and co-workers?

SEEKING THE TRUTH

Become a faith detective. Here are some resources for your own investigation.

The trailer promo for *The Da Vinci Code* movie ends with the dramatic words "seek the truth."

"Seek the truth" is actually a pretty good motto for Christians, who seek to follow the one who called Himself "the way, the truth, and the life" (John 14:6) and also proclaimed that "the truth will set you free" (John 8:32). We hope that reading this booklet and any books debunking *The Da Vinci Code* will at least make you skeptical that Brown's story is anything but fiction through and through.

But what is the truth? The truth is, the Church really isn't hiding any of this stuff, because, frankly, there's nothing to hide. But we don't want you to take our word for that any more than we want you to take Dan Brown's word for the opposite.

The truth is, there are plenty of good, solid, honest, readily available sources where you can check all this out for yourself. You can do the hard work of sifting the evidence and bringing a critical eye to anyone's claims. We learn all the time about things that are important to us, whether it be computer software, restoring classic cars, cooking or knitting, or movie or TV trivia. Why do less for our Catholic faith? (Unless a Web site is given below, all the titles are available from www.amazon.com or www.barnesandnoble.com)

The early Church

If Brown's account of the early Church has made you wonder, or maybe inspired you to try to learn more about different forms of early Christianity or how the New Testament came to be, we recommend starting with some resources by Professor Bart Ehrman of the University of North Carolina at Chapel Hill. He is a well-respected scholar who writes very well for a non-technical audience. His book *Lost Christianities: The Battles for Scripture and the Faiths We Never Knew* is clear, helpful, and fascinating. His companion volume *Lost Scripture: Books That Did Not Make It Into the New Testament* provides English translations of 47 early books, with helpful introductions. Ehrman also has done several excellent series for the Teaching Company (www.teach12.com), on cassette, CD, or DVD, including *Lost Christianities: Christian Scriptures and the Battles Over Authentication*, so if reading time is sparse, you can learn a lot in the car.

Scripture

Why not pull out the Bible and read it? What do Matthew and Mark and Luke and John tell us about Jesus? How does their view of Jesus challenge our life? What is Jesus asking us to be and do, if we are truly his followers? These are books to come back to again and again, because while they don't change, we do: We always have new insights available.

Want to know more about what Catholic scholars say about the Bible? *The New American Bible* offers splendid introductions to each of the books and very helpful notes throughout the text. *The Catholic Study Bible* provides all that, as well as a longer introduction and study guides for each book.

Reading the whole Bible is a job. *God's Word Today* is a periodical that breaks up the Bible into daily sections and offers helpful reflections and ways to pray with each passage and apply it to our lives (www.godswordtoday. com). Each month *God's Word Today* looks at a different book of the Bible; over a few years, you'll read the whole Bible, and learn a great deal about how it applies to our lives today.

Doctrine

What about Nicea and early Church debates about the divine relationship between Father, Son, and Spirit? What about the development of all this doctrine? Check out *The Creed* by Rev. Berard L. Marthaler. Marthaler clearly explains how these doctrines of the Creed developed, what they are, and how we relate to them today. We highly recommend it (like all the resources we are mentioning here).

Nothing drives our bishops crazy faster than someone disagreeing with Church teaching or, worse, leaving the Church over some doctrine without really knowing what the teaching is. And you can't blame them: Can we really disagree with something we haven't made real efforts to understand? What's the basis of our disagreement? What credible argument is behind our opinion?

So, besides Marthaler's book, read the *Catechism of the Catholic Church*. If that seems too daunting, there's a plain English version broken up into bite-sized morsels in a pamphlet series available to parishes called *Growing Faith* (www.23rd.com). Read the documents of Vatican II. Again, if the churchy language of the documents is too hard to get through, there's a series of books called *Vatican II in Plain English* by Bill Huebsch that renders the documents in trustworthy but less complex form.

Debunking *The Da Vinci Code*

Want to know more about why *The Da Vinci Code* might be enjoyed, but not trusted? You've got lots of choices. Two of the best: Bart Ehrman's *Truth and Fiction in The Da Vinci Code: A Historian Reveals What We Really Know About Jesus, Mary Magdalene, and Constantine*, and Amy Welborn's *Decoding Da Vinci: The Facts Behind the Fiction of The Da Vinci Code*. And the U.S. bishops have set up their own Web site at www.jesusdecoded.com.

Finally, what really, really, really matters...

Sometime around the year 200 A.D., a Christian named Tertullian wrote many books defending orthodox ideas. Most people today have never heard of him, but he said something that has been quoted over and over — to the point that some people mistakenly think the words are in the New Testament itself. When pagans look at Christians, he noted, they tend to say "see how they love one another."

That will always be our best response to notions like those of *The Da Vinci Code*. Learning our story and doctrine is important. They help us understand who we are and who we're meant to be. But when we face judgment Jesus isn't going to ask us where we stand on the great debates of Nicea. He's not going to judge us on whether or not we read or saw *The Da Vinci Code*. He's going to judge us on whether or not we fed the hungry and clothed the naked and took care of the sick (Matthew 25:31-46). He's going to judge us on how well we took on our baptismal life as his disciples; how hard we worked, with whatever gifts we had, to make his Body present and active in the world, to join in the great Paschal Mystery of his dying and rising for the sake of the world.

The King will answer, "Whenever you did it for any of my people, no matter how unimportant they seemed, you did it for Me." (Matthew 25:40)

We become part of this Paschal Mystery in every sacramental celebration, and we are to live it out in every moment of our days. In a poetic sense, we ourselves are part of the Holy Grail — the consecrated vessels holding Jesus' Body and Blood for the world today.

Discovering what this means and being part of it is the *real* exciting Christian adventure of our lives.